LOOKING FOR GOD

LOOKING FOR GOD

Story and Photography by Ammie Bouwman

credo
house publishers

Published in the United States by Credo House Publishers,
a division of Credo Communications LLC, Grand Rapids, Michigan.
credohousepublishers.com

ISBN: 978-1-625861-22-1

Cover layout and interior design by Frank Gutbrod
Cover font and symbol freepix.com

Printed in the United States of America

For Osa Bella
with love
Aunt Ammie

I woke up one morning feeling so out of place. I jumped from my bed, combed my hair, washed my face. I looked in my room—He was not to be found. I listened so closely. There wasn't a sound. I decided right then with one giant nod I would search near and far and go looking for God.

I went straight to my yard and looked up in the tree, but the birds in the nest looked straight back at me.

I thought God was probably not in my yard, so I hopped on a train and I searched near and far.

I searched in the deserts,
the hills far and wide.

I looked on the mountain,
both front and back side.

I searched in the rain, in the sun, far from home. I searched where the buffalos run and they roam.

I searched till my toes touched the edge of the sea. So I boarded a plane armed with only a dream. I mustered more strength and with one giant nod I continued my search— still looking for God.

I went to a place that was
different from home,

a place with a
farm where the
animals roam.

The people were friendly. I felt safe and sound. I continued my search, in the air, on the ground.

I searched and I searched till I found my way home. Up the stairs to my room, washed my face, used my comb.

It was then that I heard a soft whisper somewhere. It was quiet and loving. God's voice filled the air. "I was there in the nest. I was there on the train. I was there in the fields. I was there in the rain. I was there in the children across that far land. In their laughter and smiles and their small helping hands. I was there in the mountains so far and so wide. I was there roaming all through that big countryside. I was up, I was down. That was me all around. In the air, in the water, and there on the ground.

And even though you couldn't see,
you were always right there close to me.

In all that searching from the start I was always there, inside your heart . . .

So now I don't need to look near and far.
I don't need a plane or a train or a car.
I can stand in my room and with one
giant nod look into my heart and find
my friend God.

THE END

Made in the USA
San Bernardino, CA
04 February 2020